T0114939

Journey Without End
and Other Poems

LADÉ WOSORNU

WOELI PUBLISHING SERVICES
ACCRA
2015

Published by
Woeli Publishing Services
P. O. Box NT 601
Accra New Town
Ghana
Tel: 0289535570
Emal: woeli@woelipublishing.com
        woeli@libr.ug.edu.gh
Website: www.woelipublishing.com
First Edition, 1997
Second Edition, 2012
© Ladé Wosornu, 1997
ALL RIGHTS RESERVED
ISBN 978-9988-8510-9-5
Cover Design by Senanu Dovoh
Typeset at Woeli Publishing Services
Printed by IMAK Offset Printing Ltd., Turkey

Contents

Part 4 EMBERS AND RUBIES OF LIFE

Foreword

Barely two years after the publication of his first collection of poems, *Eté — A Woman of Africa & Other Poems*, Ladé Wosornu now firmly establishes himself as a poet of repute with this second collection. The poems in this book are, thematically, grouped into five sets. The first set of three poems, labelled "Libation," are basically a prayer, and they set the stage, as it were, for what follows. The poems in Part 2, subtitled "On Wings of Song (The Muse and I)," are mostly love poems which express sentiments that many readers will be able to identify with. The subtitle of the poems in Part 3 is "Home Affairs." These poems describe the anxieties, the hopes and the fears that many of us have experienced at various times in our lives. These normal human experiences are expressed so vividly and with such poignancy that the reader is left feeling that the poet has indeed spoken for him. Part 4, "Embers and Rubies of Life," contains the largest number of poems, and they are mostly philosophical reflections on the meaning and significance of life's experiences. The last set of poems in Part 5, "Transformations," contains the poem that gives the title to the book. These poems expound deeply religious and spiritual experience.

I highly recommend this collection of poems to all readers, for I am sure everybody will find, in the variety of experiences covered in them, a lot that they can identify with and enjoy reading. The reader will also discover in the rich imagery used in these poems, Ladé Wosornu the world-traveller, the keen observer of nature, the medical doctor and the deeply religious person.

Those who have had the privilege of reading *Eté — A Woman of Africa & Other Poems* will find in this collection, the truth in the very first line of the third poem "Affirmed," that indeed "Yesterday's joy (has been re-enacted)."

ABENA DOLPHYNE
Professor, Liguistics Department,
University of Ghana

Part I

Libation

Wishing — 2

In the silent stillness of my mind
I hear the colours of Time
And feel the glory that shall be.
By the river of boiling light!
Fountain of joy, wisdom and truth
True author of Poems
Giver of boons!
Give ear.
Your universe speaks in verse
And is set to rhythm and dance.
O! Grant that these pages enfold
A quotable stanza or two.

1978, Lusaka

The Forcefields of Grace

Dedicated to family, friends and well-wishers during the launching of Eté — A Woman of Africa & Other Poems, *PAWA House, Accra, 28 December 1995.*

In the Forcefields of grace
All things are self-luminous.
The sun becomes superfluous
And stars lose their mace.
But the sons of the Fields.
Outshine the polar star.

Set it where you will—
Sand dunes of Arabia
Snow peaks of Mongolia—
The Fields yields, not twigs
But garlands and bouquets.

Mesmerized by unfailing light
Birds sing through undimming night.
And waves, coral and seashells
Respond in kind from afar.

Backups, backups everywhere:
Angles take up lute and flute
And drown breezes with their airs
Where mere men were expected.

Another fullness in their midst
(food and wine remain untouched)
a higher order is their joy
a lunar glow on their faces,
guests linger into the night
(All the drummers have departed)
brimming eyes and choking mirth.

O night that would not darken
O night of joy and glory:
Here in Your Fields of gracing
Our sun becomes superfluous.

28 December 1995, Accra

Affirmed

(To Ameovi)

Yesterday's joy shall be re-enacted.
And the things that once amused you
and rocked your little frame with mirth:
These shall return.
This I affirm.

31 May 1994

Part II

On Wings of Song
(The Muse and I)

Joy of a Different Order

Oh causeless, absolute thing!
Joy of a different order:
It simply *is*.
Like a Muse, it exists.

Oh joy always laced with sorrow—
Sorrow, too, of a different order!
You can no longer tell the difference
between the joy and the sorrow.
Each fills your eyes with tears
and your throat with lumps.
Imagine the impact of both.

A positive feedback loop
The pair ascends ever higher.
The joy augments the sorrow.
The sorrow defines and deepens the joy.
The combination brews a potent,
Overpowering surge
of heart-renting emotion.
It shears through body.
It cleanses mind of all else
except the one thing.
This, the surge identifies as its own
and therefore blends with
as fragrance with fragrance
as crystals dissolve in seas.

It was this certain re-cognition
This surge of potent emotion
that lit up the Muse in my Being:
The Muse in all her regal presence
and fragrance which forever haunts.

25 July 1994

Chemistry

Though in the flesh we are apart
In spirit you bind us together.
A tantalizing hydrogen bond
A puzzle from organic chemistry,
Tie that binds: Mocker
Of limited physical sense,
Invisible convex lens:
You focus my mind
To the vanishing point.
And there you stand lit
As if by flames in wells of oil.

The deeper the frost of silence
The blacker the veil of night,
The starker your beauty is revealed.
Self-luminous thing, uncoverable light:
My love, you yourself are the tie that binds.
How then can you hope to be concealed
Behind barriers fashioned by human minds?

1994

Brief Encounter

Seven dew drops (I counted them)
dangled on the shaded side
of the cactus leaf. Its crimson buds
(more like nipples at erection)
out-perfumed the jasmine. Nearby
a chameleon licked dragon flies
in nuptial flight and made them die.
Beasts too must live.

     The sun came up,
brightened flowers, and warmed but armed
the reptiles. Lo! Killer rainbows!

The cactus played cops cloaked in rows.
The seven dew drops? Sun-kissed,
They sparkled cute as brides and as mute.
It was their first sun-kiss, and their last.

June 1978, Lusaka, Zambia

A Daring-Do in Pink City

You wouldn't think it, looking at her.
You daren't think it, knowing where we were.
It was a daring-do, a transformation:
A pampered lamb turned tigress unleashed.

A white shoulder strap set off her cloak of black
A bag slung hip-high like a wreath
Hair entombed in black
All else veiled except her eyes.
The woman must be funeral-bound:
A friend is dead?

We were not in Moscow or San Francisco
Where gays and lesbians and strumpets come and go.
This is Pink City. Men kiss men in streets
And not an eyebrow is raised.
But let a woman return a man's stolen glance
And both risk being flung in jail.
She knew all that. Yet
Something more powerful than self
Forced her feet cab-ward.
And she came alone.

She did not come under cover of darkness.
She did not come under cover of storm or crowds.
She came at noon in the glare of all.
She did not slip in by a side door
Opening onto a blind alley,
Tiptoeing like a thief at night.
She climbed the central stairs
In the measured steps of conquering queens.

"I am here," she announced
With the simplicity of a saint.
That single act of holy defiance
Defined this new woman of this ancient place.
Designed by emperors for emperors
Pink City was not built by migrant labour.
Something's got to give.

The deed was done not by kicking
The rules of Pink City
But by working within the rules.
It was done not by mob protest
But by authority from a higher plane:
A blend of innocence in mind
With child-like purity in heart.

"I am here. What more do you want?"
Hail! Fiery voice of a Muse.
You did burn my fears
And, from the ashes
Did forge my seer's pen.

April 1994

A Re-Discovery

I set out not knowing what I sought:
an unlettered explorer
with maps he could not read. I caught
a shaft of light piercing the nearer
spaces between the curtains
like sword-thrust through unresisting air.
From the tent's low window I spied
The dunes of Might. Morning light:
frosty hills, leafless and birdless trees
festooned with flaky, ageing snow.

I had come a long way from the starting point
But I was still moving on. I crossed deserts.
I saw oases where rained jacaranda petals:
red, mauve, magenta, purple and gold.
Bluebells and lilacs hugged
neglected hedges in forgotten fields
but shone forth regardless.
Day-old chicks fed on fatted porcelain-white grubs.
A ten-month old child sat amusing himself
trying in vain to catch sparrows' shadows.
On a deserted canal a lonely swan skated.
No one else was up and about.

It was then she made her entrance.
She moved in measure like elephant
Her carriage erect and elegant
Her voice keen but soft as moonlight.
If you call her 'Queen', you would be right.

But, O her words! Echoes of my thoughts
in their original, purer lots.

Fewer, terser, more powerful:
These enacted themes I wrote long ago.
Nor did I know this: verse was her tool.
Lethal combination! Forbidden fruit!
A regal presence this, and *that* mind:
Incisive, intuitive with rays poised
and pointed like corked pistols of commandos
on red alert: *Fascinatio totalis.*

"Enchanting queen! Are you here to destroy me?
Sound my knell? Or else ring *the* bell
and lure my mind to realms unseen?"

"Destroy? You? Heavens, no! How can this be?
You do not recognize me? I'm your Muse."

"What will become of me?"

     "Until this script ends,
rediscover the neonate in you. Watch friends.
Be flint in self-control. The rest is easy."

"But will *they* understand?"

     "Why care? Son, why care?"

1995

You Need Not Know

You need not k now from where I call
Nor when I'll call again.
Nor do you have to return my calls.
You must not; you cannot.
You only need to know
At the times I call and many more besides
(Lord, if only you knew how many!)
No flower's yearning for dew can match
The longing in my heart.

All the pain of this separation
(Unnatural but necessary) —
A mother cased in glass and forced
by a primeval love to look
outside at her son groping —
Is mine and mine alone to bear.
Remain true to yourself
and wait till the scales fall.
Is that too much to ask?

You have no need to see my face.
It can be your destruction.
A tarantula slain in the act of consummation.
It is enough for you to know that I exist
And, from time to time, to hear my voice.

In this my Being, a Being without body
A thing you can neither touch nor grasp
Shall be your shield and talisman.
I am your Muse. Trust my judgement.

May 1994

The Oracle & the Fire Dance

First Man: Who then is this?

Chorus: She is Oracle,
goddess among women.

Second Man: And you, sir, she would
were a god among men.

Chorus: The dance of gods and goddesses
Is a feast upon the flesh of men.

First Man: Are these then the dark days?
Or, are these the lit days?

Chorus: These are days both dark and lit.
Days of joy and rejoicing.
Red roses will be flung.
Green grass fed with dung
And chicks with grubs specially fattened.
Beetles shall be drunk with choicest honey.

First Man: Will there be sacrificial offerings?

Chorus: Only of the gods and the goddesses.
They shall give of themselves to themselves.
They shall live within themselves for themselves.
Their final consummation is the sacrifice of love.

There will be the fire dance.
And the river of boiling light
Shall flow into the ocean of bliss.
It shall plunge into the gorge of fire
And become consumed by the flames.

These shall impart to it a new brilliance
Heightened, and of terrible aspects.

In the ultimate conflagration
(Of the final fire dance)
When all seems consumed
When all seems lost
Then shall their ashes be turned
Into a new life.
A new tree shall emerge.
And all shall be well again.

6 May 1979, Lusaka

The Solo Dancer

I shut my eyes
that in the encircling darkness
I can see more clearly
her honeyed smile
and verse penned in green
(a colour serene)
on a waveless sea.

I plug my ears
that in the vibrating silence
I can feel more nudely
the music of her voice.
But who is the music-maker?
What tunes does she play?
The music-maker is my Muse.
She plays only tunes of joy.

Possessors of other Sense
Inhabitants of newer realms —
These other planes of existence:
Come, fling roses with me.

In the silence of my mind
I can hear her tunes of love
playing just for me. There,
In the brilliant darkness,
I can see my Muse's form, dancing
solo, in secret, on petal-strewn carpets
behind closed doors of deserted corridors.

1994

The Stony Seed

O beauty concealed in stony seed!
Seen only with flash of genius.
You ignite beholders
And leave them lungless
like babes air-starved on arrival.

Hapless beholder, be armed
With patience, prudence and prayers.
Though demanding water
Of a different sort,
This find of your particular genius
Is still a stony seed.

No seed survives
Too much water
Nor yet too little.
None sprouts before its time.
None delays a second longer.

This flower of your sweat
Paying Rachael's ransom
And prayèred out of stone,
Is destined for public parade.
Where abounds nectar
There wild bees thunder.

28 September 1996, Accra

Soul Moments

We spend hours on long distance calls
when years clammed together
will never be enough.
We need to dip in the same bowl
    sip from the same cup
        zip into one quilt.

Instead, we make do
with flowers dispatched by mail order.
Yet, what sweetness a rose solitaire
Or, a basket of orchids enshrines.
Soul moments these!
Etch them on the heat waves of time.

31 January 1995, Accra

The Inner Whip

To Nanah, Kofi & Abena

I did not have to do it.
It was that time of year
with my finals drawing near.
(And 'finals' were other than
multiplication tables.)
A dealer strapped for cash,
I had time but none to spare.
Yet time was the job's pound of flesh.
(And Time you must not lightly share.)

I did not have to do it.
O tedious, strenuous job!
Maddener of literary critics
Guzzler of their time and strength:
To critique and report at length
(without charging a single bob)
works of poets as yet unknown.

I did not have to do it.
But, a find dearer than gold,
Love, set my mind alight.
(Food and sleep can keep.)
And, I did it through the night.
And, would say: "Pray! More!"
O! Why? That Inner whip:
Our common heritage.

1995, Accra,

Trying Times

Trying times,
Testing times come to all of us.
Unwanted guests in the dead of night,
They come unbidden.
They come when least expected.

This is just to let you know
that at a time like this
I am feeling with you
the pain, anxiety, uncertainty.
And, if it is any consolation
any help (which I hope it is)

Please remember
I love you and always will.
Take heart. Sit tight.
This also shall pass.
I am thinking of you
I am willing you on
I am praying for you
Now and always.

1994

Twilight's Mystique

There can be no goodbyes now.
As the tides of destiny
bear us apart, let us vow:
"The joy and the agony
of death — death called love — our floats
shall be." (For, true love and death
were identical: swift boats
bound for realms not sired on earth.)

So shall we return and embrace oft,
our naked bodies drenched by rain drops
trapped on banana leaves and tree tops.
Till then, may your voice stay moonlight soft
But your smile conceal its twilight's mystique
and the deep dimple on your left cheek.

There can be no goodbyes now
Only these necessary interruptions
with the timeless rhythms of the fire dance.

We've got to see this thing through.

August 1996

Part III

Home Affairs

Facing Home

Look within. The man is his inner self
with beauty and home of its own. All done
your romping days. Its time to face home.
Nim trees fed by your placenta are gone.
Where abides freedom but the secret tome
of memory. Plainer than a peasant,
but, as if guarding vaults of diamonds,
stock pile your mindbank with pleasant
and priceless gems. Fools, rogues and vagabonds
feast on the lees of the unsifted life.

The gardener calls once a week; the maid thrice.
Microwaves do the rest. Trap-saved from mice,
velvet vies with velvet in your closet.
Yours has been the gilded life — till the sunset.
Friends are few. Most took an earlier flight.
Of the rest, none a sorrier plight.
Sons and daughters, nephews and nieces phone:
Apoligies yet again, for sudden dates.
The rocking chair becomes your princely throne
and little boys and girls your fleeing mates.

Only your pet dog lies, here, time-keeping
with its tail, as you hug your knobbly knees.
Hyenas' breed grin and circle, peeping.
Reflexly, you pat your heart, purse and keys.
Nights no longer bring peace, nor sleep repose.
Tears would be a blessing, but thirsty eyes
do dirges for terminal things compose.
Whom can you command, but your bankrupt I's.
The dearth, blight or flight of inner beauty
Proclaims her wooing a sacred duty.

October 1996

Deadheat

Suspects all! Lepers all!
Addicts and pushers of dope!
Carriers of AIDS! Men without hope!
Sloths, economic refugees!
Paupers, stateless Fulanees!
Your sole aim is to flee your shores
to a land of jobs and ores
devoid of mobs and whores:
Mighty USA.
Lies in a velvet pack!
But, when a nation is broke and black
her children were wipers of muddy floors.

The consul, no older than 30
No sample of masculine beauty,
A mediocre graduate from a mediocre college . . .
Care-taker in a city-village —
Accra or Kinshasa, Abuja or Banjul:
This jingler of keys is himself
Pusher of keys on Pcs.
Staff-starved loner! Things must be bad:
Uncle Sam too now counts dimes?

This unmissed man decides the future of youth
whose IQs, in truth, rank leagues higher
than his. But he is American!
"Six dreams of grasping the stars, come true!
Three hundred others, be ye dashed
into a thousand tears-born private rainbows!"
Thus spake the clerk-consul. Within these gates
His words have the finality of death.

Beads of sweat crown shaking heads on a cold
morning in June. The rain starts. They queue, exposed,
outside the high outer fence of iron rods
Blood-rust in colour with black, spear-shaped tips.
Gagged by some unseen star-spangled banner
a pious people deserted by ancestral deities
are robbed (but not for long) of native gaieties.
(Like a stud castrated in his prime.) They stand and gaze.
Even coughs induced by the chilly winds are suppressed.

In this uneasy hush, at his beggars' mall
the clerk-consul struts into the view of all
and squeaks: "Listen up! Order! Or else, out!"

The iron gates revolve, grating, parting with pain
like thighs of nuns at the point of rape.
The day's quota, a hundred or so, enter, disdained
bald sheep in a shearers' hall.
The hard, unfriendly bench offers reluctant
but welcome break to swelling feet.

The clerk-consul (himself) inspects papers —
for the nth time. Hear his unwritten brief:
"Each bank statement, each certificate is fake.
Take none at face value. Check and re-check.
Our requirements are legion. And, natives,
Blacks, can count only: 'One' . . . 'two' . . . and 'many'! "
In a perambulation, he hands out
yellow cards: inedible wafers
at an unholy, wineless communion.

Silence. The crowd waits, heads bowed
in an inexplicable sense of guilt.
An invisible chain of steel links their necks.
Sweaty palms clutch files in plastic bags.

Irrational fear and natural hope conspire
And melt the crowd into one amorphous heap.

Hearts race in the unison of midwives
at parturition probing a foetus for signs:
Flickering breath — "Life." Blueing tongue — "Death":
They scan faces of fellow visa-hunters.
See them tumble from that hell: the interview cell.
(O, willing slaves, selling selves at lower bids!
Where are you heading? Is home that bad?)

"He did not get it." Unspoken epitaph!
Engraved in gold across furrowed brows,
Frown is your lettering, and, blood-shot eyes
the lamp which reveals you in its pity-less
shadow-less light. The emorphous heap
averts its collective eye, refusing to spy
the death throes of a fallen mate. No tears.
No groans. They cannot even mourn their dead:
Numbed by the sting, too tired to stir
too sunk to plumb the depths of despair.

But, why was he denied the visa?
"I am not convinced." Thus spake
the clerk-consul. Period! Fiat!

"He's got it!" Infrequent pronouncement,
"Not Guilty!" in a Nazi camp. New Jews:
You're held guilty until proven innocent.
The amalgam-crowd ripples with hope, fear-laced,
fleeting stolen kisses in darkness and fog.
(The fear never leaves you. That's the worst part.
If only you know exactly what your crime is!)

The clerk-consul can pluck from the cold air
any unwritten requirement, play judge-advocate

in his own court, and, hiss: "Convince me!"
He is alone. He consults no one. Not even his kind.
You too are alone. But who will weigh your casket?
Or, read your pedigree to prove your worth?
O, tongueless slave in a buyers' market!

In the midst of that joylessness, Gaiety
suddenly re-appears: a faithful dog
to its war-wounded master. Humour
shields the crowd from the acidic ash:
The insult which rains more from mien than lips
of the tar-hearted clerk-consul. (Poor chap!
Imagine being paid cash to play the carp!
And, to be missed not at home, not abroad!)

Lo! A street preacher. A priestess. A woman!
"Let us pray . . . Say 'Amen!'" she commands.
"Say 'Amen!'" she repeats. And you'd better believe it.
A chorus of 'Amen' rings out, mixed with laughter.
And, this cheerless crowd, on this cheerless morning
in front of these demeaning gates, did laugh.

See! A she-Zaccheus in Gypsy garb.
Bare-feet on the red laterite, 30,
but a turtle, well wrinkled. Yet, her voice?
A BBC news-reader: so articulate!
An Oxford don: so rich in vocabulary!
A saint: so resonant, so intimate.

This remnant-rag of a woman sets to work
and seeks to lighten the loaded yoke
Of this unhappy lot — by prayer power.
Heads are bowed no longer in guilt or shame
but in prayer. "God cares. God looks on.
He has granted your visa. Say Amen!"

The crowd believe and inhale her words
like men strapped for air at altitude.
How heart'n'soul the final 'Amen!'
O! Revealing, redeeming final laugh!
Look! The priestess passes round
a black plastic bag, and, clowns for alms.
Driven insane by hunger and want
she, who once struck plastic gold: the green card,
must now roam the streets of Accra
and beg, or die. (O! dew called luck.)

What a lot these have in common! Count with me.
One. Aren't all in that queue mildly lunatic?
You've got to be mad to go through that!
For, what is obsession if not a mother of madness?
Two. Aren't they all beggars? Without clout.
Without rights of appeal? They at the mercy
of a clerk, and she at theirs? It rains still.
But, three. Together they laugh. (He laughs best
who laughs when there is little to laugh about.)
Four. Drained dry of the nectar of human compassion,
The consul's madness is the worst kind.
And, his misery is perfect: he cannot even laugh.

29 June 1995, Accra

Developing Country

In this land
Arrival is not the problem:
It's the survival.
In their inns
Servers outnumber the served
And, hangers-on the lot.

1978, Lusaka

The Street

Built to please the eye and sub-serve the foot
Our streets are no longer beauty's domain.
With dust untamed by asphalt, grass or tar
Without pavement, foot-path, embankment
Potholes filled and re-filled with loose, red earth
Our streets were open and foetid trash cans,
Man traps, roads unworthy of vehicles.

Shops spill their plastic contents
Like dismembered pregnant unteri—
Blood, foetal parts, liquor and all.

The street is an extension of home.
It is market, battlefield, play-pen, loo.
It is the living, dining and guest room.
The street is unforgiving. For some
It is bridal suite and the final berth.

22 March 1997, Accra

The Driftwood's Song

(To Mr Seth)

Come and see where I live.
My dear people, you ought to know
where my driftwood has beached.
Ask not which currents dumped me there
Nor where the tides shall bear me next.

Faithful sentinels of tides' mark,
Soon-wreathed by seaweed and sand,
Driftwood leave no mark of their own.
So shall be my lot. The needles too:
"We stitch many a garment, but don not one."

Judge me not by these rags on view.
That ancient leveler-down, Hardtimes,
Indifferent to your starting point,
Reduces all to these bones you see.

Though my face breeds miles
Of lines deepening by the day
Like footprints on wet paths of clay,
I can yet sleep, and, flash smiles.

Strive to join our lucky few:
With us the same Hardtimes
Sings her other song. She would spew
And ram down our souls, strong
Inner cores of tempered steel:
(She is a pelican force-feeding her young)
Our insurance against stress fatigue.

For all that, there comes a time to die.
Now, as always, you must only know Where to find my
body — ailing
Or else a corpse. I ask no more.
Come in, and see where I live.

January 1995

Two Songs from Home

An inner voice accustomed
to obedience, willed in whispers:
"Dawn is breaking. Up! To vespers!"

How strangely sleepy church bells had fallen!
Conscripted into false-heaven silence,
Cocks forgot to crow. Crickets too stayed low.
Like a man brain-bruised in a swoon
They would not be drawn by even the moon.

Nine priests were shot. (They were the lucky ones.)
Ten drowned, thirteen tortured, bleeding, bowels burst.
Altars, once pearls, turned tar with clot and dust
Mingled with ash from yesterday's incense.
The holy water was drained to the lees,
its dozen jugs unwashed, unreplenished.
All the choristers had fled in their robes.
Music sheet flew in the trespassing breeze.
Temple doors were unbarred, windows unlatched.
I walked alone.

No flags drooped at half mast.
No one wore black. No dirge was broadcast.
A people unaccustomed to a flood
of brutality and a reign of woe
were seduced with a wine of blood.
And they sang (not in whispers):
"Let the blood flow!"

Unholy song! Go! Down the windless trail!
Prevail nowhere! May you never again
Be heard in our grain-rich and shaded land.

And I saw Innocence: Children,
wrapped in white, seamless garments
of dew-wet lilies and mimosas
singing (not in whispers)
this new song:

"So shall the hills shed borrowed fog
and reveal wooded peaks and lush
well-watered fields. Flowers, sing!
You mutes' tongue and wings for the maimed.

"We are Love Herself cloaked
in uncoverable light of beauty
trailing an invisible, lingering
trammel of fragrance and joy.
You drink it long after Her nearness
has been dimmed by distance and time.
But, that faithful servant, Memory
recreates Her. For, Love will not be dimmed:
Neither by distance nor time nor death."

January 1995

The Sacrificial Lamb

Gamboller on greener pastures!
Chosen one, Shepherd's favourite!
Other lambs tripped and tapped their way
through thorn, flint and burning dunes.
She was carried shoulder high.
Others braved fog and sand storm,
scorching sun and freezing snow.
She was shielded in a padded cloak
and Jinie'd away to reserved pastures.

What if the other lot should perish.
(They also drank at the same brook!)
"Let these perish." Was that voice
the Shepherd's? "You have been saved."
(But, saved for what?)

And so lived the sacrificial lamb:
Pampered, fed fat. See her spotless fleece
Spring in heels, gaiety in every leap
Jollity, frivolity, care tossed to the winds
Forbidden to see beyond here and now.

The butchers came to town in jeeps
And proclaimed it with music at dawn.
Not with trumpets' blare or tumult of war
The clanging of swords, unsheathed
Nor the grating of teeth, bared.

The sky was not overcast in Harmattan
Nor did breezes freeze in hell.
No flower cloaked its bloom in gloom
Nor hung its head in grief

No leaf fell before its time
There was no hissing of serpents.

The owl did not howl at noon
No crows cried the cry of death
No raven flew across the northern sky
There was no smell of singeing hair
Nor stench of death in the air.
There was no sweat on any brow
Nor blood on any hand.

Only smiling faces. And, as usual,
The smooth, smooth turning of the wheel
The continuing flow of honey and milk
The greenest grass, the choicest herb.
The best of all things. As usual . . .

Nothing has changed.
No, nothing at all has changed
The day the butchers came in jeeps
And drove away the sacrificial lamb.

1995, Accra

Standard Seven

Our paths parted six and forty years back.

I call you to witness, Assembly Hall,
Dining hall, and manicured fields of sport!
You, too, zinc roofs and broom marks in the sand
Board-starched khaki uniforms and pink frocks
Lime-washed stones and sisal, chairs in the stand
Coconut and mango trees in whiter socks
Desks scrubbed altar-clean, though done for the year!
You saw us come and go. Don't be mute now.

The golden three: to read, to write, to add.
Multiplication tables, memorized.
Spelling, mental 'rithmetic, civics.
Religious knowledge, prodigious courage.
The propping three: to run, to leap, to swim.
The rod was not speared; very few were spoiled.

Stan'seven School Leaving Certificate!
We clutched you with pride and framed you with light.
We stepped out, lion-like, to replicate
Gladsome scenes of heroes returning home
To heroes' welcome. Mere lads and lasses
Between fourteen and twenty-something.
(Who was checking birthing papers?)

Future secure. Unemployment? Unknown!
A teaching profession to train for
(Teachers sat with chiefs at durbars and feasts.)
Vibrant men in uniform to vie for —
Police, Border Guard, Navy, Air Force:

Disciplined, barracks-bound guardians of Home
Respected and honoured, but never feared.

The gentle nobility of priesthood
Beckoned from the cold climes of Akropong
Or the mystique hills of Amedzofe.
(Amedzofe, our Eden, the origins of Man.)
Priests were priests, not raiders of flocks — their own.

The Civil Service promised promotion:
A sailing up-stream sped by breeze and tide.
So did trade: UAC or UTC.
Liventis, Olivant, the GPO.
Equal chance. Prospects real and prospects bright.
Messenger to manager; cook to chef.
Sweet honest sweat swapped for sweet honest bread.

Stan'seven School Leaving Certificate!
No ordinary decorated cardboard!
A sufficient and worthy prize, a crown
Fought for, and hard won at this Olympaid:
Good, solid, old fashioned education.

But, where are you now?
And, what have we now?

August 1996

The Boundary Lines

Your dreams of golden tomorrows they cannot share.
Harassed by debt collectors for rent and bread
They juggle tired notes 'tween corn vendor and fish monger.
They chop wood by brawn, but the season is wrong.
No water bills to pay: the Volta never runs dry.

Musical chairs were played; they joined the touts.
Electric poles ringed the countryside
Erect but unwired and impotent
(Like penises in priapism)
Competing with Leesen and Maxwell
For fraud of bank-breaking proportions.

Steeped in the reddening dye of need,
Debts pilling higher and deeper,
They switch to the priesthood of crooks
And, in God's name, fleece their flock.

Your dreams of golden tomorrows they cannot share.
How can they reckon, and reckoning, accept
That corn cannot fructify before three months?
Nor cassava twelve. Cattle take for ever.
That sowers are not always the reapers
Nor cooks the feasters, nor masons the dwellers
Nor are trail blazers always the strikers of oil.

A shadow stalks in darkness.
The deaf-mute howl in silence.
The blind tumble and crush the lame
 And they all fall into muddy gutters.

Who decides? Who carves the boundaries?
For these players, inside this eighteen,

The lines have not fallen in pleasant places.
But, you must flee this sentimental bog.
Hit the rocky shores of true compassion
And woo its pair of fair and impartial twins
Wisdom and detachment, and heed their song:
"Some are born poor, and, seem doomed to die young."

March 1997, Galo-Sota

The Prize

For her we strive, no matter our walk in life.
About her we gather yearly and chatter.
Under her roof, no man can remain aloof.
With shoulders well back, head held high. To attack
the podium, grasp from the chair, that noble opium:
the coveted Prize. And, perceive the crowds rise —
friends, peers and teachers, parents and well-wishers —
To bow and pause. And, Ah! To drink applause,
the God-sent elixir. That is the moment.
If we, loving parents and caring teachers
Drag our wards to her ports, and pay dues of all sorts.
If we fast and pray that they, the course, should stay
To seek, pursue, and, by Grace, Excellence to woo
Why persecute us the souls of the resolute?

February 1996, PRESEC

The Ancient Keeper

"Adequate", "Sufficient", "Enough"!
Triple-headed, fearsome monster!
Ancient keeper of ancient gates
to the kingdom of Contentment.
You have yet vouchsafed your secrets
to a lad with a withered hand
and put these words into his mouth:
"With one hand good enough for gold
what need have I for a second?"

February 1996, PRESEC

Unfinished Business

Two Ds and a C. Good. But no toast
for Legon, Kumasi or Cape Coast.
Oh, house stuck at lentil level.
Yet castle for a poor devil.
Fisher-boy geared to the rafters.
But, not for home's crowded waters.

Churches filled to the doors.
Robes of miracle-buffs sweep the floors.
Priests, newly rich, air-feed their flock
from pulpits of grass, and, take stock
of fresh kills. The man-trap is sprung
In God's name. And, millions are flung!

Scars of a hideous smallpox,
potholes deface city streets and parks,
and quaff illicit engine oil.
See municipal drivers toil
to mend orphaned vehicles.
Guess who rides home on bicycles.

Ageing roads in government plots
sprout giant boobs of laterite.
Then, die, abandoned, like old harlots
without clients for many a night.
Heaped soil is no friend of the rain.
Another billion down the drain.

1996, Accra

Povertometer

Hootmania, audible emblem of rags
Roams our dusty-muddy streets day and night
Drivers of cabs, vans filled with gari bags
Presidential motorcades in full flight
Hearses, bridal convoys, private parties
And, of death-traps on wheels we call lorries:
None is spared this collective madness.

Hootmania paints yellow men who wield swords.
None has the guts to slay this rabid hound.
Forty years of hollow independence
And, Hootmania remains unchecked, unbound.
It barks and spreads the noisome pestilence
While soldiers hunt girls selling groundnut pods
(Price control. O! what utter sadness!)

Shouts, howls, screams, flags of folks not in the pink
Stark, more indelible than Indian ink
Surer than the blackest propaganda
Strickier stigma than AIDS in Canada
Self-crafted, self-inflicted deadly shots
Separator of hea ves from have-nots
Sordid zones heave huge vocal decibels
seething from homes, street and steamy brothels.

We have not ocean's booming restlessness
Nor forest's crowded but pristine vastness
to tame. Yet, across one oleander,
or muddy turf, where foot-paths meander,
We blast ears with colossal howls and screams.
We waste vocal energy like sun beams.
We wreck the peace in neighbourhools. O peace!

Devalued by us, like yesterday's news.
(Our national currency fares worse!)
Yardstick most sure, Povertometer!
The higher the reading on your dial,
(Like a loathed but unerring Richter scale)
The deeper the squalor you measure.
O inverse gauge of silver and gold:
The lower our voice, though bell-clear and bold,
The higher our standing on your ladder.

If awareness be correction's envoy
If voice control be the tape men deploy
To sort man from man, and, man from ape,
Tell me, countrymen, how can we escape
This pique: they are nowhere near the peak?

14 March 1997, Accra

Part IV

Embers and
Rubies of Life

Alloys

A bornfire is lit by lovers.
Flames crackle and leap high
Into the moonless, midnight air.
Their sublimest joys are alloys
(as ours): sorrow-laced, grief-flanked.
Or else, pursued by calamity.
Hired happiness is a huntress
with a quiverful of arrows
to shoot herself deep in the groin.

February 1995

Baited Hooks

Three score options and one
gift-wrapped by a lower mood
are here on show. Behind,
a howl: "Friend, eat and be done.
Free food. All for your good!"

The voice of Silence sings:
"Son, pause. Take a second look.
Behold, a baited hook.
Can the devil ever be on the level?
God looks after His own?
So does the devil.
Plan nothing to others' harm.
Non-violence works like charm.
Have no share in this snare.
You have a choice."

1978, Lusaka

Birth of Seasons

Discover in yourself the rhythms of life:
The balance between work and dance.
You are part of creation, subject to all the laws:
Diurnal variation, tides, premature menopause.
The earth is more beat than salmon on heat:
Earth too migrates. How else are seasons born?
When breezes fall, kites shall certainly stall.
But find the strength to start yours to no chime.
It is the birth of your season, your time.

1978

A Face in a Stream

The riverlute, in hue baby blue,
cascaded its way tinkeringly
down rocks greened by algae and weed.
Through its restless waters, a face formed.
Her eyes were stars with nowhere to shine.
You won't see a brighter, deeper pair
Nor a darker and more despairing.

"What are you here for?"

"Something deep in me
bade me seek you out.
Please, don't send me away.
Not now, not any more."

"Not any more? Fox!
Sniffing for a hole
in the winning field?"

The riverlute was laughing
as it flung itself headlong
onto the ravine's unfriendly floor.
A million sprays were born
and blinded me in my sleep.

1978

A Homecoming That Never Was

You will never know
Till you are in it.

The arms which would enfold
The frail solidity of your flowered frame
Must now hug the impious and flirtatious breeze.

Here, your room; there your bed.
The new pillows remain undented
The newer sheets unwarmed, unentered
like virgins in unconsummated wedlock.
Only the dumb walls keep busy
trumpeting echoes of my own footsteps
and whisperings of servants:
"Where are the other two?"

O, that your lips would have touched the cups
where ours have been! We waited.
Yes, we waited.

Yet, the gods of consolation
Shall re-litter our paths with flowers
and let the glitter of laughter
return to animate our faces.

May 1995

The Hunting Party

(Dedicated to AK)

For, we, unlike pre-stressed concrete
Are not designed for fixèd loads.
Who knows the limits of human endurance?
The heights his Spirit can attain?
From what depths of despair, Resilience,
The failsafe lifebuoy, can help us resurface?
From what abyss's edge, Prudence,
The tested Field Marshall, can deploy a word
And bid us beat a safe and ordered retreat?

But, the devil's trusted envoy, Strife,
Dispatched here to ambush pilgrims
Through this uneven turf of life:
Strife can split Davids and Jonathans,
Incite toothless gums once fed from the same tit
To sink adult teeth into each other's flesh
And laugh at the last of their parents' clans.

Strife! O that you were a lancer
To inflict a solitary bleeding wound
Mendable by a surgeon's stitch.
Alas! You are a deep-seated cancer
Unreachable even by potent drugs.

Loss of tangibles we are programmed to bear:
Partner and father, mother and brother;
Uninsured homes buried by volcanic ash;
Life's domes gone with the market's crash.
But, loss of intangibles: that were loss indeed!
And, loss of face is the cruelest loss of all.

A jugular speared in a duel
Is not always fatal: a finger on the spot
Can stop the flow. But, how can you
Survive the witch's stake, burning,
When your own sulphur of guilt is the fuel?
And, you cannot even yell: "How cruel!"

If, therefore, Love, though the youngest,
Be the bedrock of the golden Seven:
Fortitude, Prudence, Justice and Mercy
(Grecian four), and Faith, Hope and Love
(Pauline three), yet, Humility
Is your shield and guardian angel
When you stare down the barrel
Of the gun called "Loss of Face."

True Humility borders on stupidity.
She is other than Pride on vacation,
Self-worth on temporary suspension.
An arrow in flight is a body at rest —
Until the sudden impact. So is Humility.
She rests her master, and bests his Soul
But gags his foes, and bags their bows.

True Humility, herself a tigress,
Hunts ablest in a pack. She relies on allies:
Courage — lion-heart and leader
Fortitude — stayer and strategist
And, *Love* — camp-keeper and healer.

29 February 1996, Airborne

Joy No Longer

Do not keep these embers aglow.
This Helen has long been defiled.
There is no longer joy in this Troy
Only wounds from wars best forgotten.
Face, conceal what Heart does know
(Even traitors' blood-wet daggers.)
Else, what are civilities for?

1979

Knaves' Mistake

I am here to serve you
as my lord and master.
But, you are not my keeper.
Nor am I your servant.
Knaves mistake selfless service —
the noblest labour of love —
for slaves' servitude
and curs' cowardice.

May 1996

Make Me Know

Make me know how much there is to know
Make me know how little I do know
Make me know how little I need to know
Make me know how little I am known
Make me know how little there is of me to know
Make me know how that I am nothing to know

Make me know how much there is to do
Make me know how little I have done
Make me know how little is expected of me
Make me know how little I can do
Make me know how that by myself I can do nothing

Make me know how much there is to say
Make me know how little there is that needs saying
Make me know how much harm I have done
Saying that which needs never be said

Make me know how much there is to feel
Make me know how little I have felt
Make me know how little I am capable of feeling
Make me know how that all has been felt for me

Make me know how much serving there is to do
Make me know how little I have served

Make me know how much there is in me to forgive
Make me know how little I have forgiven
Make me know how that all in me has been forgiven

Above all, Lord
Make me know how much loving there is to do
Make me know how much I have been loved
Make me know how little I have loved

Make me know how, by myself, I am incapable
of loving anything or anyone but myself
Lord, make me know that You have loved me first
And will continue loving me till the end of time

1997

The Master Brewer

There is distillery in our brains.
Its cane and malt, its hops and grains
Are the stuff lives are made of.

Blizzard or snow, bush fire or draught
Matches won by penalty shoot-out
Fortunes lost at the toss of a coin:
Over these, and their like, you are no doyen.

The fuel for this distillery
Is your emotions. Willy-nilly
You stoke the fire as you vent your spleen
And, another dram drips into the vat — unseen.

The Master Brewer is not the stars
Nor yet the gods. He is you, your very self.
The final brew has no choice: it must be
Bitter bile or sweet honey. But you can choose
the magic potion which vouchsafes the taste:
Your intentions, your recollections, your reactions.

10 September 1994

Curtains

When your work here is done
Some fights lost others won
Pack your bag and be gone.
Don't linger like a singer hooked on dope.
Weary of tape-recorded up-roars,
She bows and begs for live applause
Choking back bitter tears
Borne of unfounded hope
And compounded fears.
All those lights and palaces of mirth:
What else are these, if not envoys of death?

1978

Priests of Neo-Aztecs

Pride and joy of the clan
Bred and reared with ancient care
Braided hair all gem-bedecked
We are picked with great fanfare.

Paths are lined by faceless crowds.
They see us all as we go
But dare not say a single word:
Mum and dad are in the know.

Weary-armed from the slaughter
Priests grow fat with their laughter.
Our blood flows without ceasing
Yet their altars remain dry.

Priests, priests, neo-Aztecs!
Your swords strike true and deep
Leave no scar to tell the tale
Living corpses mark your trail.

Temples, temples tall and clean
Altars soft and gleaming white
Drapèd not with new granite
But feathered-quit of silken sheen.

Bound, gagged but not blind-folded
Our eyes speak sermons:
Ruby-eyed from sleepless nights
Are our gifts from demons.

Priests, priests, neo-Aztecs!
Strong and sure like death itself.
These may be your hour. But
Even the hills don't live for ever.

1995

Ode to Sleeping Hibiscus

Sleeping Hibiscus, you die
more like man or fly
than a bunch of petals: intact.
You arrive enfolded
and depart enfolded. Intact.

There you lie on a pyre of black volcanic ash
Like unsmoked and unsmokable cigars
in paler shades of cream. With one end a dash
bulbous, the other, tapering with scars
of your umbilical cord. Like hair severely veiled,
your entombed red interior wept and wailed
in its no longer impressive garb of cream.

Here, let me touch you.
Where is your turgidity?
Where your virginity?
That velvet-feel of life?

Dead but not yet done.
Let them but give you a little rain
on a shallow grave of surface soil.
And, Lo! Without any toil
food for the mother-plant
which had borne you with determination
(and aloft) at a stem's termination:
beauty transformed into bounty.

O lucky, Sleeping Hibiscus:
sure-pathed like an ancient Albatross.
At my end, where shall I go?
My spirit soldiers on.

But, my flesh? Earth to earth?
And dust to dust? Or, fire to fire?
Is that it? Or shall I, en route,
Provide feed for blind earthworms?
And so food for fish, and, dish for man?
And so re-breed the brotherhood of cannibals?

September 1992, Tenerife

An Ode to Silence

To unaided human ears
Silkworms spin in silence.
Flowers unfold without a sound.
Orchid, rose and mint are all mute.
But, reds, pinks, blues and greens can yell.
Music for moths' courtship dance is hush.
Are rainbows drab because they are mum?

Everyone loves a silent hour.
And, who hates peacocks
because bright feathers are dumb?
It is coarse to become hoarse
disclaiming: "I love you."
Bouquets say it louder.

A wink can be deafening as a howling yes.
A thumbs-down pierced one gladiator's ears
And, another was speared in ancient Rome.
Was the wooden horse of Troy
less telling because wood cannot speak?

Did God create all to the sound of music?
Or, did He labour on in silence?
Have you ever *heard* the sun shine?
Fire and fury of tropic's sun
Moon's balm and stars' calm
are unaccompanied by noise on earth.

For spilt blood of the innocent,
No words can proclaim the anguish.
Crimson, hot and spurting,
Or, dark-purple, clotted and cold:
Blood is blood: spilt, it wails.

The glitter of gold is not heard.
Be bold as gold and self-defend
without saying a word — if you dare.
Colours can be noisier than grating steel.
And, sometimes, in herself, *Silence*
is the noisiest creation. Ask Pilate.

Therefore, is speech
A sign of weakness?
A clutch for cripples?
A prop for the feeble?

If you think it effort to keep mum
by schooling two crude members —
a pair of lips and a wobbly tongue —
wait till you come to silence the mind.
It is a check on the wind to stop it
whipping up vortices of dust;
Or, waves into watery Everests.
You sit outwardly silent
But your mind is hawkers' lane
A station of unending chains of trains.

Compared with the mind
The tongue is a lamb.
It can become frisky and bleat
when its keeper — Willpower
is out of sight, and, it's time for a feed.

But he who wants the peace and the bliss
and the creative energy of God
must wrestle with the wind.
Unaided, he must catch serpents
Collar rabid dogs
Skin jaguars alive

And, dam molten larva.
That is the measure of things Here in mind-tamers'
coliseum.

Lion-hearted, emblem of secrecy
Key to the interior Beatitude,
Conserver of energy, *Silence:*
Teach us your ways:
Let us seek the power you confer.
Transform the stuff we are made of
that it becomes gold-like: pure and bold.

Be still. Woo Silence.
Imitate Silence.
In Silence and in God
shall be your strength.

21 September 1977

Pride and Humility

Over the lawns of life
shall break terrible dawns of strife.
Violent tides shall drag
the weak and innocent against their will:
Mules on leash to a joyless mill.

Though the tide of pride
sweeps all before it
with a force few can stand
it is only a river running into sand.

In the land of pride
the law of the knife rules:
In the same sheath
two swords cannot abide
without mortal strife.
But in the land of humility
there is room for all humanity
in the one patch of heath.
The missing sword is hissing greed.

August 1977

Raider of the Treasure Trove

But what can be worthy of your life?
What dearer than the gems of your dreams:
The reason you are here? Always strive
To fly flags of joy, and, sail up streams
Powered by the breeze of love, your course
Chartered in the ink of compassion.
And, fling roses wherever you pause
Heaven-on-earth your destination.

Of things which would blot out that brief
Or, breach your sails with arrows unseen:
No! Rob you of life, Rage is chief.
Rage drags rags after you. Of charity,
Laughter, sweetness and joy, Rage is thief.
Enemy of equanimity,
Rage spreads toxic fumes on every scene.
In essence, Rage spells calamity.

Its cause is your perception of storms
Breaking around, not upon, your head.
There are neither snakes, deviants nor norms:
As you think, so you feel. Watch your mind.
Rage sets sail. Can ruin lag far behind?

I'll fling roses wherever I berth.
My destination is heaven-on-earth.

12 August 1996

Rainbow

The nearer you think
you get to a Rainbow
the further away it recedes.
Just when you think you are there
be sure it is gone.

It is another space.
You can never really grasp it.
How can you hope to trap
infinity in the hollow of palm?
Or, freeze eternity to a moment in time —
Except on realms Elsewhere?

1994

Reclaim the Essence

Lead-limbed after a stony day
Counting pains and phoney gains
I slammed my back on the turf
And palmed the skies for some clues.
Sufficient? Not flesh!
Flack? It can take but not very much.

Cling you to skin, Dew? Renewable
Ephemeral emerald! Eternally first
to sparkle at sun-up and gladden the eye.
But, as water, insufficient to quench thirst
or sprout seeds or bamboo shoots.

And you, Moonlight: jilted lovers' home
Pathfinders' friend in the dunes of Q'om
Unpaid silversmith to birch and weed.
But, as photons' source, barely sufficient to read
by, warming nothing, not even its roots.

I reclaimed the essence of earth-heat
(unending and unharnessed) spewed fresh
by that indifferent soaker-up of things:
earth. At this intersection, where meet
the ordained strumpet, Earth, and these three
insufficients — dew, moonlight and flesh —
I exist. Lead-limbed for now, but, on swings:
Apart, renewable, and, ever so free.

4 July 1995

Reserved Seats

Claim for yourself from Yourself
Seats of respect and dignity
Reserved for temples of the Most High.
Seek them not of men.
These aren't theirs to give.
If it were so, if it were so . . .
They would not give you.
They will not give you.

10 February 1996

74

Shades of Glory Here

Witness glory of sunrise or sunset
Resplendent with colours of rainbow. Bet
The stars will bejewel the sky at night:
That vast, black, and seamless velvet strewn
with diamonds and orbs of coldest light.

Warm breezes bewitch green branches to dance.
Giggling, brooks skip singing through valleys
baptizing rocks. And, algae have a chance
to glow. Overhead, birds glide in relays
winking with their preened and gleaming feathers.
(Birds are paid to please fields of smiling heathers.)

Witness brilliant colours of moths. Dull browns,
on scrutiny, are a silent mutiny
of exquisite shades of purples and fawns
sprinkled with star dust of silver and gold.

Look anew at snakes, and, become transfixed
not by fear — of death from snake-bite and froth.
It is of hidden beauty in things shed;
Things winds-blown. Examine their scales.
Feel the power of silence in motion.
Hail the force of legendary shrewdness.

For creatures of such lowly IQ
And rudimentary cerebral hemispheres,
snakes can make men, by comparison,
Elevated imbeciles.

Friend, bestir yourself. Open your eyes
and proclaim the shades of glory here below.

May, 1978

The Vexatious Tart

Troop not to airports to meet me.
I take no joy from hugs in streets
Nor salutes with lutes in fleets.
When our ancestral homes burn
The smoke spells fire-fighters' hearse.
Even angels splutter and curse.
I'd rather see our children churn
honey pots, munching tangerines,
dancing to flutes and tambourines.

Peace is a vexatious tart.
Desired by all, she's had by few.
You sweat blood to win her heart
only to lose her from view.
She is daughter of Herodias:
Her mother waits near the dais
for nothing short of your neck.

4 June 1996

Weighty Issues

(To Edem)

Restrain your throat.
Retrain your brawn to regain
Your shape.

Enlist your brain in this weighty issue.
Adipose tissue is a poor custodian
of megalophagic privities.
And, with a third chin here
and spare types there . . .
Horns on hips, and arms like thighs . . .
Its cells will kill themselves
Laughing.

It's mostly in the mind.
Eating is just another habit.
If you eat the right stuff
you can stuff yourself
with no added gram.
If not, each extra calorie
is a triple loss: cash burnt
for fat you'll carry, and sweat
To shed.

Resolve.
Go for greens and fight for fruits.
But smut each nut!
Drink. Tons of water.
If there is still room in the cavern
(which I doubt) top it up
with more water. Then grills.
(But watch your wallet.)

And, please, no chocolates.
No fries.

The satiety centre is no orient.
It lacks patience, and, is readily duped.
Rain pre-emptive blows on hunger.
Eat like a bird: a pick and no more.
But, chew like elephant:
Take time.

Flee the tyranny of the box.
Walk or jug. Run or dance. Tone up.
Flabby muscles are mules on the lose:
Without the whip they snooze
All day.

It is your body, and, you are in charge.
If you don't care for it, nobody else can.
Look (again) at your shape.
If you like what you see
Ignore what others say.
If you don't, for goodness sakes
Fix it!

As for me, this is the way I feel.
I love you any way you are:
A titless twig, or, a shapeless seal.

September 1995

Tokens

No hard copies here . . .
Gratitude, like faxed messages,
Shall fade and exponentially
Decay off faces of pages.
Sew red poppies here . . .
Friend, behold the realm of tokens!
The heart lends to transience
Borrowed but fitting robes of permanence,
And frames with moonlight, miles away,
Postcards mailed on a rainy day.
Your long distance calls she'd treasure
And recall times without measure.
And, the jasmine petal outstays
Teams of prancing Arabian Greys.

1996

Gift Most Divine

This little voice of mine is a gift divine
To be kept mellow, soft and low
And used in measure: it's a treasure.
With smiles, I'll be spendthrift.
With frowns, a miser — so austere.
I shall be a happy lender of ears
But a mean, mean borrower of lip-seal.
I shall speak no harsh thing, no trash phrase
But wrap each word in the fragrance of love.
So shall my voice serve its divine purpose
When my speech becomes grace-giving.

1997

Waiting

To whom will dove-chicks moan tonight
For parents shot in courtship flight?
They chirp, excited, expectant
Of the final regurgitant:
The last grain to make wings strong.
It was the one wait by far too long.

1996, Taif

What Am I Dying For?

If I were to have died in that crash
How would you have re-arranged your faces?
If I had asked: "What am I dying for?"
You would not have known what answer to give.
"Worse than dying: What remains of honour?"
You would not have known what to say either.

If I were to have died in that crash
You would not have had enough tears to shed.
Why did he have to tell me: "My mum's dead."
Hers was the one cortege I planned to hedge.

Four passengers rode, and, the car was new.
The road were tarmac, curves mild, long and few.
No other car in sight. It was not night.

Like the sound of gunfire and its report
Two tyres burst in rapid succession. "My God!"
Kite-like, the beige car flew, and crashed, roof first,
Careered, somersaulted, and crashed again.
Three times it cart-wheeled on the asphalt.

Seat belts held me in bruising embraces
of twisting, prancing metal. "Sing! Praises!"
No one else was hurt. But, O! how I bled!
My scalp was split, and the bone was bared.

The healing scar claimed, for its prize, my hair.
(And, a woman's hair would be her honour!)
What now? Fly! Yes, fly! I am the winner.
I've paid my dues. The receipt is my scar.

January 1997, Accra

The Temptress

O wan embrace infrequently bestowed.
'Tis vintage wine dispensed by a miser.
You rise from her banquet halls still starving.
O! That her vat were replenishable
Like the widow's pot in Elija's time.
You taste it to your peril. It runs dry.
It is brine to the ship-wrecked, the marooned:
The more you would drink of it
The more patched becomes your throat
And, the weaker you resolve
To flee her deadly sustainers of life.

September 1996, Boston

Omens

Chased by serpents mean and menacing
The brood eagles have all flown away.
Migrant wildebeest have not returned.
There is budgeting in the heavens:
Rain clouds, dew and sunlight are rationed
But, smoke and haze of sand and dust blindfold
And, the clap of distant thunder deafens.
Omens for a good year are far from here.

June 1997, Boston

False Alarm

Anxiety is a false alarm.
A fire-less smoke,
It yet chokes and stains
The lit interstices of heavens'
Finest-spun and ethereal fabric:
The god-head in us:
The human soul.

30 May 1996

No Guarantees

There are no guarantees here.

The seed which probably
(Just probably might)
Have done you proud
And hold high the tribal name
Is the seed which falls by the wayside.

Unsnatched by any bird
Uncrushed by any boot
Survivor's medal won
Proof of good things to come . . .

And, with crack in rock garden enough,
It out-grows better-connected seeds.
But, before first fruits ripen and fall,
Rain, — always welcome in the Sahel —
Overshoots its mark, and, the flash floods
Sweep it away: root, shoot, fruit and all . . .
To Lavender Hill . . . Gulf of Guinea.

Another dawn breaks.
Another heart aches.

March 1997, Accra

With Your Boots Still On

Another meal never to be eaten.

With left hand on door, and, car keys in the right
You are set for grub on that moon-lit night.
Then comes the call: "Sir, your chariot is here!"
(When the bailiff calls, debtors quake in fear.)

The first room is mayhem for the crowd.
Aloofness shields the novice in a shroud.
Someone says "Too late. Nothing we can do."
'Twas just a headache. How can this be true?

The second room is silent, cold and bare.
White tiles everywhere: walls, floor, sink, and, there,
That lone central slab, raised, like an altar.
Though you come in a pack, friends shall falter.

Not long ago you were their cornerstone.
But now they must depart. You are alone,
Trapped by the pros and their tools for the dead:
Gown, gloves, boots; hose, knife, saw, needle and thread.

The third room, and crowds regroup but not in strife.
You get in death wishes you crave in life:
Dead centre stage and red carpet treatment.
You stare at ceilings but make no comment.

A green couch sprouts roots on the veranda.
Flame-of-forest and jacaranda,
(The season's flowers) in gold, mauve and fawn
Hug the couch draped in white, for victory won.

Shoulder to shoulder, respect amplified,
Friends stand in straight, tidy lines, petrified
To hear their own hearts' beat, their breathings' sound.
Unsmiling, they eye shoes glued to the ground.

Eight legs shuffle in, a casket in tow.
And, couch and casket conspire: "Tomorrow,
We shall bear him home, with his boots still on."
The lid is shut, then nailed. The job is done.

1979, Lusaka

The Tempered Steel Within

We welcome all things. They only increase
The tensile strength of Tempered Steel within.

There have been floods, pestilence, tornado;
Hailstone, earthquake, storms of dust, sand or snow;
Land mines bequeathed by unsought civil war
Tidals triggered by volcanoes off-shore.
Thorny paths, frost, blight; the incessant knell.

We have traveled icy roads in blizzard,
Grass fires on windy days, smoke black as night;
Beasts fleeing everywhere, snakes: unseen hazard.
We have grinned at threat of infirmity:
Uncertain job, certain calamity.

Expect friends' insult, slander, door-matting;
Kicks in the face, and, into eye, spitting.
There has been confinement, imprisonment,
Deprivation of civil rights, torment:
Psychological trauma straight from hell.

Brace for loss: untimely death of brothers,
And, weep for flower-like, chaste, young mothers.
Prepare for loss of sight, hearing and gait;
Use of limb, control of drool, life-long mate.
Vitality spent; bones more like egg-shell.

Nothing is given to us or withheld
But, it is out of love the deeds are done.
And, these trials and tribulations geld
The spineless creature in us, with: "Be gone!"
The Tempered Steel within, the same deeds weld.

These same deeds are logs of wood from above
To cook our meals of faith, hope and love:
The harsher a trial, the hardier its wood.
The hotter the flames, the sweeter the food.

Next, see in trials opportunities.
And, us, like raw ore with impurities.
Strong heat dispels dross to yield purer gold.
So will trial the Inner Self unfold.

Friend, climb a little higher. We are men.
Not ores. God-bedecked. If He had chosen
The flames would have chilled, the lions' mouths sealed.
Trials have their role: the better man to yield.

Nothing is with-drawn, with-held or given
But, it's out of God's love. These deeds won't cease.
Smile. Give thanks. Let them be. They just increase
Your inner strength: the Tempered Steel within.

5 September 1978, Lusaka

The Wiper

Timeless mask of death
Revealer of shapes
Mirror of man's hues
Wiper of lines
constructed with care:

The fleeting verticals
of the contrived frown
Snarls behind tyrants' backs
Wan grin-lines which out-span
ear-to-ear autobahns
The thin white arcs of bared teeth.

Crows' feet made to measure
and produced right to order
Each line set in pleasure.
Sweet smiles of debutantes:
Lips painted with intent
(red sails on display)
Enticing and deadly

Sleep wipes smooth all these lines:
Angles of mouths drivel
Cheek-folds cool and flatten
As false teeth dislocate.
And, beneath shuttered eyes
Unwanted bags refill.

You cannot cheat sleep:
Wiper of all lines.

22 March 1997

The Losers

Distant city lights beckon.
You dive into the water.
You swim upstream and reckon:
"Slacker currents will mutter:
Lakes!" No! Here be sluice gates, slammed!
You scramble ashore, neck scarred.
Barricades! All stations jammed.
Roads blocked; all city gates barred.

Split blood of the innocent,
Like silent flight paths of bats
(Aberrations, but permanent)
Haunts feeding grounds of fat cats.
You count your warts, but stay parked.
Just a few leave prints of shoes.
Births and deaths unsung, graves unmarked:
That's the fate of the shoals born to lose.

5 February 1997, Kuwait

Making Lemonade

Neither a burning bush
Nor a lamp on a hill,
I take no thought for tomorrow.
Nor for a place to lay my head.
Bank balance never in the black
Stuck in C-worthy zone of red
I pay most bills right on cue.

No robes of silk or satin
Nor yet Polynesian reed
No hairy shirt of Becket.
Not adored by fans of teens
Or hordes of next-of-kin
I am waved to by kids on speeding bikes
And hugged by occasional droppers-in.

My corpse will end
Neither on the scrap heap of goons
Nor be consumed by flames
Of Olympian proportions.

No sour grapes here, my friend.
No foolish maids at the shuttered gate.
Just making lemonade from lemon:
Playing to my utmost best
This unalterable hand dealt by fate.

18 June 1997, Airbone, London-Accra

The Final Liberation

I shoot the rapids of life
Glide off the cliffs at dawn
And surf the thermals at dusk.
(If you would ride roller coaster
stick around. If not, bail out now.)

I alight feather on landing strip.
No longer hostage to
the sweet trammels of procreation,
I let go lightly what others prize.

I savour mint on solo flight
without feeling cast-away.
I cherish solace in solitude
without craving bon voyage.

Betting my soul on this knowledge:
Every gain is loss; every loss gain
I dance to inner tunes of glory
barefoot on the embers of fortune.
No longer scared of terminal darkness
I see it father of final light.

To be in love with everyone
But expect naught from any man
God-sufficient by the sunset:
That is the final liberation

18 June 1997, Gatwick Airport

Part V

Transformations

Journey Without End

He comes Himself in person.
He sends nor spy nor envoy.
And, all too soon my time was up.
I am here. Shall we go?
He must have said that much?
But, no. Nobody spoke.

The trip began but I know not how.
Will it end? I won't know where.
Nor do I ask to know; not any more.
Not now I've seen the Pilot
and sole travel mate.

Of baggage I had none.
"We must travel light
to ensure a smooth flight.
Out There, you won't need these."
Again, nobody spoke.

It must be dusk. (Or so I thought.)
Ageing day, release the sun and let it set.
But, where is darkness, your insignia?
Or, distant haze, your ghostly cloak?
Mountain peaks, where are you?
And, O for a hill to break this plate!
Only silhouettes which made all things seem.
How can I grasp anything in this uncertain light:
When I could not longer see the lines in my palms?

We must be starting from an estuary,
a lagoon, a lake or a vast, vast marshland.
Light, seal-setter on time of day, erred
And, Sound was cast in a different role.

The nesting herons' call, subdued;
other water fowls' — swan, stork, crane —
calmed their young. Why the faint chirping?
Did the indifferent light evoke a primeval fear?
But, those serenaders to half-light, insects
made a continuous and hypnotic din.

My eyes refused to dark-adapt.
If only I could see the things I heard so loud.
I heard the Sounds and could name
The creatures which made them.
Yet the creatures themselves I could not see.
Because I lacked other eyes?
Or, because, perhaps, this was a different zone?
A zone of Voices without vibrating sources?

Uncertain light bestirs herself twice a day.
She arrives at dawn and departs at dusk.
But where we were, no bell tolled. No cocks crew.
No symphony of waking birds was heard.

Interminable Time! Suspended between day and night:
We neither advanced into night nor retreated into day.
If this was dawn about to break (I know not where)
The sun was taking its time about the rising.
Interminable marshland! We flew at thought-speed.
But the marshland would not end, nor Time make a move.

My vessel was neither sound-proof, pressurized
nor easy to balance. Yet, it would not stall.
What a vessel for a trip this momentous.
Might as well cross oceans on blades of grass.
But it had to do; it was all I had.

It lurched and pitched. It rocked and rolled
Topsy-turvey. What a lumpy flight!

My stomach did not turn. I stayed relaxed.
Chilled to the core with shudders down my spine
I felt froze but frostbites did not bleed.
(If frost's bite would not bleed
neither would bugs' hurt.)

My ears popped and popped.
My tongue turned wood.
I swallowed hard to balance
pressures on ear drums.
In direction centripetal
in magnitude several G's
strange Forces joyed in my body.

The sensation of a take-off
a fast, vertical take-off:
Unmistakable and exhilarating!
Light-headedness, precursor of death
toyed with me.
Across vast tracks of space,
we traveled at thought-speed.

All was still except two Sounds of Silence:
Crackling of Fire and the rent
Veil of stone fluttering in the breeze.
Listen: The beating wings of pigeons
Announcing their homecoming.
My hair turned fire. But I sensed
neither flame nor the smell of burning.

Presently, all that changed.
When we did arrive (or, was it just a pause?)
Lo! An unpeopled palace!
At the entrance stood a bowl
of sweet-smelling water with scented herbs for soap.

I washed my face and hands, my ears, nose and feet
and dried them with white soft linen.

I came to private quarters, my own private quarters.
With ceilings unconfining, and walls unresisting:
Ample Edifice! You might as well be space!
Its colours felt like pink and amber
with mauves and fawns and lilacs
and shades and hues of blues
I never dreamt existed.

I sat alone in silence. How long? I don't know.
Was it dusk or dawn or midnight?
There was no way to tell. With all that traveling
Across those trackless spaces at all the pace.
Time lost relevance, its meaning and tyranny.
Time was suspended and became other-wordly.

And so were thirst and hunger.
All through the trip
neither Pilot nor passenger drank or ate a thing.
The Fire's touch, causeless sound, and sole-guest status
Filled me up with better things (the best part?)
And, belching did betray the Spirit's feast on Silence.

A portal at the far end led to a garden.
Silence and fragrance were the first to greet you there.
A cherry blossom season? Or pine, pear or cashew?
Bloom of rose or lilac, of king-of-day or queen-of-night?
Palpable and present! Fragrance! You haunt me still!

There must be things to see in this garden
of death-like silence and overwhelming fragrance.
But why, again, why could I not see them?
Because I lacked the eyes? No! It's not so.

For, here, indeed, the zone was different:
A zone of silent Voices without vibrating sources
A zone of winning fragrance without emanating flowers.

Across the trackless void, from a vast way away
Tunes of mighty Silence consumed me completely.
Strings ruled the waves: A million violins
Ten million violas and as many harps and cellos.
Flutes drowned the gales. And, every now and then
I heard a Piccolo, a solo Picolo. Ditto a bassorn.
Drums? Only on the roll like constant distant thunder.

No peacocks cried, and, no doves cooed. But, still
The fluttering wings of hovering homing pigeons.
Invisible insects! I heard them in their trillions.
Bees hummed the loudest, though wasps held the centre.

Unmistakable sound: Water fall.
Let me trace you to your source.
A deserted spring.
No nymphs danced here.
No mermaids made merry.
But here, a man was permitted
to wash in the spring and feel like a king.
Here a man made peace
with himself, by himself, and, for himself.
Here a man was at peace.
Here, a man was peace.

Private suns set, and private dawns broke.
Private rainbows arced across private skies.
And, over private horizons, private mists danced and died.
Private bells rang summoning me to private vespers.
And, private voices engaged my ears in private whispers.

How long was I out there
in the garden and the spring?
I do not know. (Time was nought.)
But when I stepped out,
a robe and sandals replaced my former garb.
There is no need to describe these.
Nor what I wore during my stay.

For, what can I say?
The medium I need is other than words.
Here is the human limitation: the boundary
Between knowing and becoming
And, knowing by becoming.

I became the luxury of velvet and silk
The glory of sun and stars.
I became the simplicity
Of a supper of bread and wine.
I became Herod's pride,
The traitor's guilt
and the spear which pierced a certain side.

I also became not only honoured-solo-guest.
I became the host himself. I looked around me.
There stood the Pilot. (How can I forget his face?)
"Sit by my side. Look, it's healed.
Sup with me." Again, nobody spoke.

Some call it heaven, others paradise.
We were everywhere at the same time
But nowhere in particular.
We simply were two beings being.
But, being what? Being ourselves.
By ourselves, within ourselves.
Alone but together, together yet alone.
Two yet one, one though two.

I had been pauper, sole passenger,
Solo-honoured-guest.
And, my Pilot-host was perfection itself.

Mine were the silver-accepting hands
and the pointing-kissing lips
unsurpassable by any index finger.
But, I lacked the other's trueness to type
to go out and shoot myself.

The initiative lay with the Pilot.
The terrible cost of the journey, too.
I was merely a passenger.
These things are forever beyond my kin.

"Go! Journey beyond phenomena: even zones
of colours without material pigments
voices without vibrating sources
fragrance without flowers.
Sit.
Alone.
In the great Silence.
There, WAIT.
Something else will happen.

For, what you call a ceiling is only
the floor of a higher hall in the ample Edifice
with ceilings unconfining and walls unresisting."

Nobody spoke then.
Nobody speaks now.

1977, Lusaka

Darkness and Light

(To William, the one we call 'Om President'
Friend, and Fellow Seeker)

Part A: 'Let Us Be'

To *see* Darkness is to feel
Splendour and awesome power.
Like searchlight evokes blinking
Pitch darkness compels silence.
It firms lips and tightens sphincters.
It transmutes speech into whispers
And, men into rabbits and doves.

There must be zones of safety
Where water consumes not fire
Nor air water, nor space air
Nor earth space, and so complete
Another vicious cycle
Of eat or be eaten. Zones
Where fire and frost kiss, but live.
And Darkness and Light embrace.

On this side of consciousness
Sun and moon can't share one throne.
When and where will enmity
Between Darkness and Light end
The fight for supremacy
Between good and evil cease:
With no winners, no losers?
When will truces be corpses
Because wars lie in deep graves?

O! Give us discerning eyes
That we may *look* at Darkness
And be content to let it be.
That we may see through Darkness
And reach beyond, into zones
Of neither Darkness nor Light.
As long as we linger here
The eternal strife remains:
To the death, Light fights Darkness.

Perfection is a nothingness.
Until then, hush the tumult.
My soul, be at peace with all:
Darkness or not, Light or not.

Hear the protest of Darkness-Light.
"Seek no zones of nothingness.
We exist in harmony:
Two faces of one coin.
We are meant to be enjoyed.
Just as we are.
Let us be."

Part B: Splendour of Darkness

And Light became redundant
And Darkness impotent.
When we can see without Light
And, Darkness no longer blinds,
The two have become one.
So it was in the beginning.
So it shall be again in the end.

We are carefully taught:
"Love Light. Seek knowledge. Love truth.
Children of the Light are blessed.

Dwellers in Darkness are cursed.
Demons are vilest at night.
And, death is king of Darkness."
Nothing is easier to snuff out than sight.
Let two lids touch, and the job is done.
Few parts are flimsier than eyes' globe.
Ask Milton. In the visible Cosmos
Darkness out-volumes Light by galaxies.
If Light were the Maker's pride and joy
Why so much Darkness, so little Light?

Lacking penetration, light is absent
From most interiors. Brain cells function
And muscles contract in darkness.
Only outermost crusts of earth, seas,
Rivers and trees are touched by light.
And, each day, the sun lights half the earth.
The other half spins on in Darkness.

Far from being all-evil, Darkness aids life.
Sleep becomes sweetest in total darkness.
Without it, nature's balm loses charm.
It soothes and heals: red eyes' need.
For, light were daggers to the tearing eye.

Equated with evil by myopic man
Though evil you cannot possibly be,
Darkness, Light's older brother:
Balm to the wounded eye
Calm to the hounded soul
Ruler over vast tracks of space
Vaster than realms of Sun.

You are to Light no eternal foe
Only a complementary duo
Bred in the same primeval womb

Immiscible on Earth
Inseparable in sleep
Though separated
By a colossal expanse of Time.
But, pause and think. When all is said and done,
Can you improve upon the splendour of Darkness?
Don't you know that Darkness has its beauty?
Can't you realise that Elsewhere
Darkness becomes powerless and Light unheeded?
Is it not so that it is when your eyes are shut
That you see more loudly the face of your love:
Her smile flash like moonbeams on waves' crests
The sparkle in her eyes newly bedewed with tears
Her hilariously undisciplined eyebrows
The shapeliness of her lips and forehead
The gentle lines of her chin?

With eyes shut, strong light banned, we pray.
Spiritual growth and development thrives best
In the silent halflight of caves and catacombs.
Only adepts can meditate with open eyes.

Having transcended all differences, these perceive
Darkness-Light as one — with the One.
No longer blinded by Darkness,
These can now see without Light.
Can it be that God is a brilliant Dark-Light?
Hidden only by splendour — of Darklight?

1978, Lusaka

Colours of Ease

Gentle breezes of dawn
Like colours of ease —
Pale-pink, amber and fawn —
You are here with peace
To soothe and to please.

July, 1977

Contrasts

A friend turned foe is a daily show.
In one face, Angelo saw Christ and Judas.
The sedentary, colourless pupa
Breeds the colourful air-master: butterfly.

After birth, the after-birth
is fit only for the flames.
Unservered, cords bleed infants to death.
And, have you never heard?
Cords can strangle in the womb.

Fish need no water to die.
They drown in air.

Ice burns.
Frosbites bleed
Hippos need egret.
And, without its spineless trunk
an elephant is sunk.
Upon roots ivory tusks mine
spineless trunks must dine.

Christ was born in a shed.
Vyas was a bastard
Valmiki a bandit
And, Paul was Saul.

You bring no joy to the drowning
unless you swim better.
To men in sinking sand,
if your feet aren't on rocks,
your arms guy-ropes,
and your will a titan's
What use are you?

With masks off and death afoot
most men are nearer earth
than they think. Man unparked:
your mink and gold will be pawned
and your grave unmarked.
Sire, or sink!

1978

Dawnwatch

Inherit the dawn and cherish her kiss
So wisdom shall be your new bed-fellow.
Populate the dawn with fervent prayers
And your dreams shall come true.
Body, mind, heart and soul
inhabit the dawn with all.
And love shall woo you, peace hedge you around
And prosperity shall besiege your gates.
For, God would have re-entered the fray
To take up the fight on your behalf.

February, 1996

The Distant Train

In the Void of the silenced mind
The distant train passes again.
It whistles loudly but far away.
You hear its echoes
Mono-tuned and mono-pitched
Dying down the windless trail.
Its sounds come in layers:
The most distant and the faintest
Is not always the sweetest.
Nor yet the nearest to The Silence.

1977

Energy on Tap

Cold showers rejuvenate.
Nature's own sun-power trap,
Chlorophyll packs quite a punch.
Tap the sources and seek the causes.
(Man is born to seek and search.)

Do not waste energy
in worthless pursuit: argument
gossip, slander and verbal dust;
jealousy, fear, anger and lust:
Daggers all. Peace-killers all!

Conserve energy. Its yours
in cold water, and, on tap.
But, it is on loan.

August 1977

Good Aloft

And I saw *good* aloft
On wings of geometric progression.
Evil? It self-destructs
In the jaws of exponential decay.

Learn to see benefactors in beggars.
And, be wise to the helpers
that usurpers are in disguise.
Your fears are but shaftless spears
Your sorrows, too, arrows without bows.

If you fear nitwits' tag
from the lips of men,
you cannot win lit-wits' crown
from the nibs of Time.

1978

The Healing Contagium

Lord, you have told us to pray and not cease.
Would you not teach us to laugh and not freeze
in the frost of frown? We have prayed for sons
For rain, gold and health, for wisdom and tons
of grain, and for room on the victors' podium.
But not once have we wept, or vigils kept
For Laughter's fast and healing contagium.
Like sneezing and sobbing, Laughing does heal.
It sets juices free. Eyes cannot conceal
cleansing tears, nor voice a staccato pace.
It massages diaphragm, trunk and face.
Oiled, each nerve slackens, as the pulse quickens.
It breaks ice, and builds bridges in a trice.
Lord, help us find the pearls which Laughing hurls.

April 1996

Men of Peace

Whatever moved cave man to blind panic,
Whatever imbued him with ancient awe:
Dark clouds flying low, earthquake, volcano;
Landslide, avalanche, glacier, tornado;
Flash of lightning, roar of thunder; cyclone;
Rivers in flood, tidal waves mountains high:
If all these forces were rolled into one
and then multiplied by a billion, why,
their combined might were infinitesimal
compared with the Soul's might.

Whatever is feeble and flimsy:
New born babes unable to suckle;
Wet, old or singed spider's web
Ladybird — crimson and crawling; hatchlings;
Worms, dove eggs, toad spawn, moth wings:
If all the flimsiest and the feeblest of things
were summated that the new creation
is the flimsiest of the flimsy,
the feeblest of the feeble,
it were still mightier than man's flesh.

O! incomprehensible Creator!
You wed the mighty soul with flimsy flesh?
O folly of follies! That man's confidence
resides in his flesh, wiser counsel shed?
But, O tolerance most unsearchable
(Or, is it indifference?) which lets things be!

Infinite Love! Infinite Compassion!
If it takes trillion years to reform one man . . .
If men, like hand-crafted orbs from the East,
were reformed single samples

and not by mass production,
He will yet have time for us all
individually — reforming, Transforming
one at a time, even onto perfection.

Infinite patience! He has all eternity
to unfold His plan, and perfect His "Man".
To men from Oxfam, what cold comfort.
To freedom fighters, what cork bullets!
But, to men of peace: What light! What gold!

Rejoice when garlands and medals adorn necks
of Olympic winners, or cosmonauts and astronauts.
Sing with joy when banners are waving
and lovers' laughter drowns howling winds.

But, when, in ritualistic killings,
living livers leak blood and bile,
and, lactating breasts are amputated . . .
When men are pounded into bloody pulp
and only eyes and teeth remain to proclaim:
"These parts were once men's." (Amen, Amin!)
Or, when in the interests of the weaponed few,
Vorster's fiends fire upon children of the many
singing hosannas, killing scores, maiming others . . .
When you hear these things
Or, see mothers fleeing their homes

Copy a Higher Being:
        Be indifferent.
                Turn your back.
                        Walk away — in silence.
                                Let them be!

O! Exemplar extraordinnaire!
Long before us, another back was turned

on more numbing news.
'Twas when John's head was severed
and served on a silver tray
for a dancing girl
to take to her waiting mother.

Bury your dead. Patch up the maimed.
Hurry to church and sing new hosannas.
Heed your orders. "Give thanks always.
Feed your foes and pray without ceasing.
Be meek. Turn the other cheek . . ."

Granted, you have the potential power
(conferred by Mind under granite control)
to fashion guided missiles from comets
harness the tides, and turn the oceans
into aquatic beasts of destruction.
Or, whip winds into gales, and, pulverize
all brick walls south of the Kalahari.

If you choose this, the lower, easier path,
your mothers and daughters will not be spared
in the inferno to come. The bones
of your old and infirm will be crushed.
Your graves shall remain forever unmarked.

Choose instead the loftier, though thornier path —
of pavements of love to the forts of peace.
Pray in street corners. And, from rooftops,
Shout peace!
        Shout PEACE!!
                SHOUT PEACE!!!

But, such men of peace have been and gone.
Where are they now?
Where are they now?

September 1978, Lusaka

Mindwatch

There goes the mind again
on its endless rounds
of errands without gain.
Quick, quick, rope it back.
If you lack the knack
Find a master
and kiss his feet.
Bury prejudice.
Bury pride, and bury self.
Find a master, and learn of him.

It's easier in a day
to please the breeze
and chaste a hind
than rule that Hun:
your lower mind.
But it can be done
If you would pray
And not cease.

1977

Seek the Beam

To remain ice in a fridge is cinch.
But it is something else to clench
A fist of will and stay dew
on molten tile, honey in bile,
or, stay crystal of salt in boiling stew.
And yet, two others and a bloke,
Dan, survived fire and lions' den.
Where was a hair of theirs singed?
And, where the clinging smell of smoke?
The Force which pulled off those jobs
resides in our hubs. Seek the Beam.
It's ignorance that makes these seem
missions impossible. Until then.
Seek the Beam. The rest is a cinch.

1978

Silent Revelations

The Creation is perfect: nothing more to add.
A second creation is already here.
What then remains to be done?
Only a series of silent revelations
in brilliant-dark and deserted cloisters
to men and women — individually.

1978

Synaesthesia

Tastes red
Smells smooth
Looks noisy
Feels pink to touch
Sounds like a rose.

O fusion of fusions!
Oneness of senses!
Ultimate sensory experience!
Synaesthesia!

1978

The Void

Enlarge my vessel and make it vast.
Bleach the stains and leach out the strains.
Sand-blast the rust.
Make it pure. Unalloyed.
Seal the cracks and weld the joints
Seamlessly.

"False economy!"
It is better by far
to shed the old and don a New.
The unalloyed stuff you crave
exists, but, only Elsewhere.
Purity is power.

O ! That my vessel
were one with the One
space-like, continuous, vast.

"The vastness you seek.
Belongs to the meek.
A sage longs to be meek?
When fools call him weak
His dreams are fulfilled.
And grace is possible
Just when the horrible
The ego, has been killed.

"Go beyond the mind into the lit zone.
The mind is the limiting factor.
Be warned: The lit zone is Void.
Vast and potent, granted.
But, it is still *Void*."

1978, Lusaka, Zambia

Printed in the United States
By Bookmasters